wok
perfection

HINKLER
BOOKS

wok
perfection

Food Editor
Ellen Argyriou

Creative Director
Sam Grimmer

Project Editor
Lara Morcombe

First published in 2004 by Hinkler Books Pty Ltd
17–23 Redwood Drive
Dingley, VIC 3172 Australia
www.hinklerbooks.com

ISBN: 1 86515 764 3
EAN: 9 781865 157641

Printed and bound in China

contents

an introduction to wok

The wok is reputed to have come into being around 2000 years ago when the Chinese first learned to beat metal thinly. Its design, remarkable then, and even so today, is considered to have produced the most versatile of all cooking utensils.

The wok, even revolutionised Chinese cuisine, for previous to its introduction, meat, vegetables and cereals were stewed together in large three-legged cauldrons stood over an open fire. With the ability to heat the wok to a high heat, Chinese cooks soon discovered the flavour of seared meat strips and combined them with vegetables and sauces, creating the wonderful stir-fries and fried noodles dishes, fried rice and deep fried spring rolls, to name just a few delights in a long list. One utensil transformed a whole cuisine.

choosing a wok

There are many woks from which to choose, from the traditional cast iron with rounded base, to stainless steel and enamel lined with rounded or flatter base. Electric woks and woks with non-stick surfaces are also available. But with all modern applications, the traditional cast iron woks, without doubt give the best result. They heat more evenly and quickly than 'modern' woks, but they do need more care. Woks may have one long wooden handle or 2 curved handles placed each side that can be metal or wood. It is best to look for a wok with wooden handles as the metal handles get very hot. You may insulate the metal handles to a comfortable degree by winding a good layer of insulating tape around them.

Large and small woks are available but it is wise to buy the larger wok for a little or a lot may be cooked in a larger wok.

caring for a wok

The modern woks available will come with manufacturers instructions for care and cleaning according to materials used, so follow their instructions carefully.

cleaning and care of cast iron woks

When new, the cast iron woks have a protective coating designed to prevent rusting during shipping and storage. This must be removed, and the wok washed and seasoned before you can cook in it.

1 Fill the wok with hot water and add 2 tablespoons of bicarbonate of soda. Place on the heat and boil for 15 minutes to soften the coating. Tip out the water and while the wok is still hot, scrub off the coating with a scourer; a plastic one is best – do not use metal. Wash the wok well with a mild detergent, not an abrasive powder, and dry well. The wok should never be scoured again.

2 To season the wok: heat the wok to dry it out after washing, then wipe all over the surface with wads of absorbent paper towels dipped in peanut oil. The paper will colour brown at first, but continue the process with clean paper and oil until there is no further colouration. Rinse the wok with warm water, dry well and oil the surface with a fresh wad of oiled paper. The wok is now cleaned, seasoned and ready for cooking.

care after cooking

It is important to maintain your wok in good condition.

1 Soak the wok to remove any hard cooked pieces of food. Remember we can not scour the food away as the surface of the wok will be scratched.

2 Wash thoroughly with hot water only, scrubbing with a dish mop or plastic brush, never with a metal scourer or powdered abrasive. Dry the wok thoroughly (placing over heat is a good way to be sure) then coat the inside of the wok with a thin coating of oil to prevent it from rusting. When storing, never place any metal objects in the wok, they may scratch the surface. If possible hang the wok by the handle.

cooking in a wok

As the wok is designed to heat quickly to a high degree it is important to have all ingredients prepared, measured, out and lined up before heating the wok. The following steps will guide you.

1 Measure out all liquid ingredients and place in small bowls or cups. Mix or combine any sauce ingredients. Blend thickening agent, eg, cornflour, if using and have ready.

2 Slice, chop or grate all meat, vegetables and flavouring ingredients.

3 Line up the prepared ingredients on a tray, in order of use from left to right. Place the tray to the right of the burner. Have needed utensils ready.

4 Place a large plate or bowl nearby to accommodate the cooked food being removed, which will later be returned to the wok.

how to stir-fry

Stir-frying is the technique mostly used in wok cookery. The food is tossed continuously to allow all pieces to come in contact with the hot metal of the wok for a few seconds at a time. The best utensil to use for this is a special wok spatula called a chan. It has a curved end, which fits into the curve of the wok, allowing total contact. Slide it down the side of the wok and under the food, then flip or toss the food over allowing the top pieces to fall to the hot base. You need to work quickly.

adding oil: It is important to heat the wok first on high heat until very hot. Turn down the heat to moderately high and drizzle the oil around the inside wall. As the oil runs down to the base it will heat and also grease the sides of the wok.

adding meat strips or cubes: Add only a portion of the meat at a time. Stir-fry, as explained above, until rosy brown and remove to a plate. Repeat with the next batch in the same manner. If needed add 1 or 2 teaspoons extra oil before adding the next batch of meat. If meat has been marinated, drain well before adding to prevent the meat stewing and toughening. Cooking the meat in small batches also prevents the meat from stewing as the heat stays high. Overcrowding drops the temperature of the wok.

1 **adding vegetables:** Add the firmer vegetables first as they will need longer cooking, eg, carrots, celery, bamboo shoots, followed by the softer vegetables such as broccoli, zucchini, capsicum, snow peas and lastly shredded greens, bok choy and cabbage. Return the meat to the wok and toss well to distribute evenly throughout.

2 **adding sauce and thickening:** Push the food up the sides of the wok to form a well in the base. Pour the combined sauces and blended cornflour into the well and stir until it bubbles then stir-fry until all the ingredients are coated with the sauce and are hot. Serve immediately.

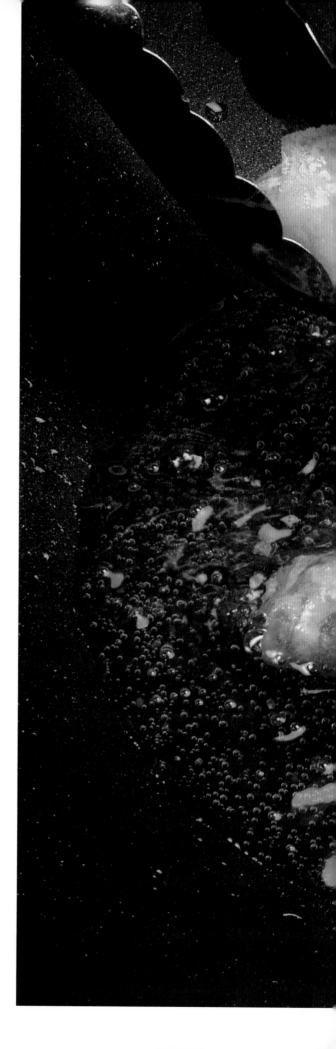

cutting vegetables and meat

spring onions: (green onions) may be cut straight across into rounds. For garnish they may be cut with the knife at an angle making a diagonal cut.

carrots: look attractive if cut diagonally. Carrots may be grooved down the long side in 3–4 places then sliced thinly. They will look like flowers when sliced.

onions: Small round onions are cut into quarters or eighths to form wedges then the layers separated to look like petals.

cutting into strips: Cut the vegetables into 6 cm long pieces then slice lengthwise. Stack 4 slices then cut through the stack into 3 cm wide strips.

slicing meat: For a tender result meat must be sliced across the grain. Purchase the meat in a thick piece or 'nut', not a slice. To slice pork and beef fillet finely, place in the freezer for an hour or more until it begins to firm. The meat will not move under the blade of the knife allowing straight, thin slices to be cut. Cut slices into thin strips if needed.

deep-frying in the wok

The wok is perfect for deep-frying. Because of its shape, you achieve the same depth of oil with much less oil than a deep fryer. A wide surface area means more food may be cooked at the one time.

1 Heat the wok on high heat, turn heat to medium high and add enough oil to be 2.5 cm deep. Heat until a haze appears; it won't take long as the wok is already hot.

2 Place in the food, 4–5 pieces at a time, and cook until crisp and golden turning once. Remove and drain on absorbent paper.

3 Turn off the heat and allow the oil to cool before removing.

wok safety: It is best to use a wok ring when deep-frying, to ensure the stability of the wok on the gas jet or hotplate. Never leave the wok unattended when heating oil; it may heat quicker than you anticipate. Don't forget the wok was designed to heat quickly.

pork

balsamic pork stir-fry

ingredients

2 teaspoons olive oil
2 cloves garlic, crushed
500 g (1 lb) pork fillet, trimmed, cut
  into 1 cm thick slices
1 red capsicum (pepper), chopped
1 green capsicum, chopped
½ cup (125 ml, 4 fl oz) orange juice
4 tablespoons balsamic vinegar
freshly ground black pepper
125 g (4 oz) rocket or watercress leaves
steamed rice to serve

serves 4

i

preparation time
10 minutes

cooking time
6 minutes

**nutritional value
per serve**
fat: 2.2 g
carbohydrate: 1.9 g
protein: 11.5 g

1 Heat wok over a high heat. Add oil and garlic and stir-fry for 1 minute or until golden. Add pork and stir-fry for 3 minutes or until brown. Add red and green capsicum, orange juice and vinegar and stir-fry for 3 minutes or until pork is cooked. Season to taste with black pepper.

2 Divide rocket or watercress between serving plates, then top with pork mixture. Serve immediately. Serve with steamed rice.

quick pork stir-fry

ingredients

500 g (1 lb) pork stir-fry strips
2 teaspoons cornflour
2 tablespoons soy sauce
2 tablespoons peanut oil
2 cloves garlic, crushed
375 g (12 oz) pack frozen stir-fry
vegetables
1 cup (250 ml, 8 fl oz) bottled stir-fry
sauce
serves 4

1 In a bowl, combine pork strips with cornflour and soy sauce. Cover and stand for 10 minutes.

2 Heat wok to very hot. Add 2 teaspoons oil and a third of the pork and stir-fry until brown all over. Remove pork, cook remainder in 2 batches adding more oil as necessary.

3 Reheat the wok and add 2 teaspoons oil and the frozen vegetables. Stir-fry for 3–5 minutes until cooked but still crisp. Return pork to the wok and toss to combine. Pour in the sauce and continue to toss until all ingredients are coated and heated through. Serve immediately.

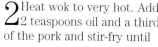

preparation time
5 minutes, plus 10 minutes standing

cooking time
10 minutes

nutritional value per serve
fat: 6.1 g
carbohydrate: 4.7 g
protein: 10.2 g

1 Rinse the fresh noodles in hot water and drain well. In a bowl, combine fish sauce, chicken stock, sugar and pepper and set aside.

2 Heat wok and add 2 teaspoons oil. Stir-fry garlic until fragrant. Add half the pork and stir-fry to medium done. Remove, cook remainder adding more oil if needed and remove to a plate.

3 Add more oil, stir-fry onion for 1 minute. Add noodles, bean sprouts and stir-fry until hot. Add the cooked pork, and stock mixture and toss to heat through. Add spring onions and coriander. Serve immediately with lime quarters.

stir-fry pork with bean sprouts and noodles

ingredients

450 g (14 oz) yellow or white fresh noodles
2-3 tablespoons fish sauce
1 cup (250 ml, 8 fl oz) chicken stock
1 teaspoon brown sugar
$1/4$ teaspoon white pepper
500 g (1 lb) pork stir-fry strips
2 tablespoons peanut oil
3 cloves garlic, crushed
1 onion, sliced
400 g (13 oz) mixed fresh bean sprouts, well washed
3 spring onions (green onions), cut into 1 cm lengths
12 sprigs fresh coriander
4 lime quarters
serves 4

i

preparation time
15 minutes

cooking time
10 minutes

nutritional value per serve
fat: 2.9 g
carbohydrate: 13.8 g
protein: 9.4 g

cashew pork stir-fry

browned. Remove and repeat with remaining pork adding extra oil if needed. Remove.

2 To the wok add 2 teaspoons of oil, garlic and onion. Stir-fry until onion is soft and golden. Toss in the capsicums and snow peas and stir-fry for 2–3 minutes.

3 Add the pork and toss to combine with vegetables. Push mixture back to form a well and add the sauce. Stir until it boils then quickly toss to coat all ingredients with sauce and heat through. Serve immediately sprinkled with roasted cashew nuts.

preparation time
15 minutes,

cooking time
10 minutes

nutritional value per serve
fat: 7.7 g
carbohydrate: 4.4 g
protein: 11.8 g

ingredients

2 tablespoons peanut oil
75 g (2$^{1}/_{2}$ oz) cashew nuts
500 g (1 lb) pork stir-fry strips
2 cloves garlic, crushed
1 onion, diced
$^{1}/_{2}$ green capsicum (pepper), diced
$^{1}/_{2}$ red capsicum, diced
$^{1}/_{2}$ yellow capsicum, diced
10 snow peas (mangetout), halved
sauce
2 tablespoons fish sauce
2 tablespoons oyster sauce
$^{1}/_{2}$ tablespoon brown sugar
2 teaspoons cornflour
$^{1}/_{2}$ cup (125 ml, 4 fl oz) chicken stock
serves 4-6

1 In a bowl, combine the fish and oyster sauces, sugar, cornflour and stock and set aside. Heat wok on high heat. Add 2 teaspoons of the oil and cashew nuts and toss until golden. Remove and set aside. Add a teaspoon of oil and half of the pork, stir-fry until well

pork stir-fry with snow peas

ingredients

500 g (1 lb) pork stir-fry strips
2 teaspoons cornflour
1 tablespoon rice wine or dry sherry (optional)
2 tablespoons soy sauce
2 tablespoons peanut oil
2 cloves garlic, crushed
1 cm piece ginger, chopped
1 small red chilli, deseeded and sliced
6 spring onions (green onions), cut into 3 cm pieces
180 g (6 oz) snow peas (mangetout), halved

sauce
2-3 tablespoons oyster sauce
1 teaspoon sugar
½ cup (125 ml, 4 fl oz) chicken stock

serves 4

i

preparation time
15 minutes, plus 10 minutes marinating

cooking time
10 minutes

nutritional value per serve
fat: 4.6 g
carbohydrate: 3.7 g
protein: 11.2 g

1 In a bowl, combine the oyster sauce, sugar and chicken stock and set aside. In a glass bowl, combine the pork with cornflour, rice wine and soy sauce. Marinate for 10 minutes.

2 Heat the wok to very hot. Add 2 teaspoons oil and half of the pork and stir-fry for 2 minutes until cooked and browned. Remove. Add 2 teaspoons oil and remaining pork, cook as above and remove from wok.

3 Add garlic, ginger and chilli and more oil if needed and stir-fry for 1 minute. Toss in spring onions and snow peas, and stir-fry 2 minutes. Return the pork and stir-fry to heat through. Pour in sauce and toss well to combine. Pile into serving bowls and serve immediately.

pork and squid stir-fry

ingredients

150 g (5 oz) cleaned small squid hoods
2 tablespoons peanut oil
350 g (11½ oz) lean pork stir-fry
1 medium onion, cut into thin wedges
  and layers separated
1 teaspoon freshly grated ginger
½ cup (125 ml, 4 fl oz) chicken stock
2 teaspoons soy sauce
2 teaspoons honey
2 teaspoons cornflour
1 tablespoon water
150 g (5 oz) yellow squash, thinly sliced
100 g (3½ oz) baby english spinach leaves
steamed rice to serve
serves 4

1 Gently score into the flesh of squid in a diamond pattern with a sharp knife or cut into medium strips.

2 Heat half the oil in a large wok over a medium-high heat. Add half the pork and stir-fry for 1–2 minutes. Transfer to a plate and repeat with remaining pork. Add squid and stir-fry for just 30 seconds and remove.

3 Heat remaining oil in wok and cook onion for 2 minutes. Add ginger, stock, soy and honey and bring to a gentle simmer. Blend cornflour and water and add to the wok. Allow to simmer and thicken liquid. Add squash and cook for 2 minutes. Add pork, squid and spinach. Stir to combine and cook for 2–3 minutes or until leaves just wilt. Serve with steamed rice.

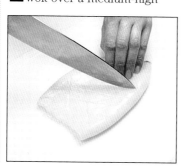

i

preparation time
15 minutes

cooking time
10 minutes

**nutritional value
per serve**
fat: 4.6 g
carbohydrate: 2.8 g
protein: 10.8 g

pork and coriander stir-fry

ingredients

1 tablespoon chopped fresh coriander
2 tablespoons finely chopped coriander
   root and stem
1 teaspoon freshly grated ginger
1 teaspoon chilli paste
500 g (1 lb) lean pork stir-fry strips
1½ tablespoons fish sauce
1 tablespoon fresh lime juice
½ teaspoon brown sugar
3 tablespoons vegetable oil
1 medium red onion, cut into wedges
100 g (3½ oz) button mushrooms, sliced
100 g (3½ oz) shiitake mushrooms, sliced
200 g (7 oz) snow peas (mangetout),
   trimmed and sliced
deep-fried lemon grass threads to serve
noodles, cooked to serve
serves 4

i

preparation time
20 minutes, plus
10 minutes
standing

cooking time
10 minutes

**nutritional value
per serve**
fat: 6.2 g
carbohydrate: 1.9 g
protein: 11.4 g

1 Combine the coriander root and stem, ginger and chilli. Rub into pork and stand for 10 minutes. In a glass bowl, combine fish sauce, lime juice and brown sugar, and set aside.

2 Heat a large wok over a medium-high heat. Add 2 tablespoons oil then half the pork and stir-fry for 1–2 minutes. Transfer to a plate, cover and set aside. Repeat with remaining pork.

3 Reduce heat to medium, add remaining oil and cook onion for 2 minutes. Add mushrooms and snow peas and stir-fry for 1 minute. Add the pork and toss through. Pour in the dressing and cook for 2 minutes while tossing. Serve with cooked noodles and fried lemon grass.

pork and pumpkin stir-fry

ingredients

1 tablespoon vegetable oil
500 g (1 lb) lean pork strips
2 onions, cut into thin wedges,
  layers separated
2 tablespoons thai red curry paste
500 g (1 lb) peeled butternut pumpkin,
  cut into 2 cm cubes
4 kaffir lime leaves, shredded
1 tablespoon palm or brown sugar
2 cups (500 ml, 16 fl oz) coconut milk
1 tablespoon thai fish sauce
serves 4

1 Heat the wok on high heat. Add half the oil and pork strips and stir-fry for 2 minutes or until browned. Remove. Add remaining oil and pork and cook as above.

2 Add the onions and stir-fry until soft. Stir in the curry paste and stir-fry for 1 minute.

3 Add the pumpkin, lime leaves, sugar, coconut milk and fish sauce. Stir, bring to the boil and simmer for 3

minutes. Return the pork to the wok and stir-fry for 2 minutes until heated through. Serve immediately.

i

preparation time
10 minutes

cooking time
12 minutes

**nutritional value
per serve**
fat: 8.4 g
carbohydrate: 4.4 g
protein: 7.6 g

pork and pineapple with basil

ingredients

4 red or golden shallots, peeled
2 fresh red chillies
3 cm piece fresh ginger, peeled
   and chopped roughly
4 kaffir lime leaves
1 stalk fresh lemon grass, tender white
   part only, finely sliced
1 tablespoon tamarind concentrate
2 tablespoons lime juice
1 tablespoon water
2 teaspoons shrimp paste
1 tablespoon dried shrimps
350 g (11¹/₂ oz) pork fillets, cut into
   3 cm cubes
1 tablespoon vegetable oil
1 teaspoon palm or brown sugar
1¹/₂ cups (375 ml, 12 fl oz) coconut
   cream
¹/₂ cup (125 ml, 4 fl oz) coconut milk
2 tablespoons thai fish sauce
¹/₂ small fresh pineapple, peeled
60 g (2 oz) fresh basil leaves

serves 4

i

preparation time
15 minutes

cooking time
18 minutes

**nutritional value
per serve**
fat: 9.5 g
carbohydrate: 2.8 g
protein: 5.1 g

2 Heat wok over a medium heat. Add oil and pork and stir-fry for 5 minutes or until fragrant and pork is just cooked. Stir in sugar, coconut cream, coconut milk and fish sauce. Simmer, uncovered, for 8–10 minutes or until pork is tender.

3 Slice the pineapple lengthwise and cut into 2 cm wide strips 5 cm long.

4 Add pineapple and remaining lime juice and simmer for 3 minutes or until pineapple is heated. Stir in basil. Serve immediately.

1 In a food processor, place shallots, chillies, ginger, lime leaves, lemon grass, tamarind, 1 tablespoon lime juice, water, shrimp paste and dried shrimps and process to make a thick paste. Add a little more water if necessary. In a bowl, place the pork and spice paste and toss to coat pork well.

beef and lamb

lamb stir-fry with noodles and capsicums

ingredients

4 tablespoons oyster sauce
1 tablespoon dark soy sauce
2 tablespoons clear honey
finely grated rind (zest)
    and juice of ½ lemon
250 g (8 oz) medium egg noodles,
    fresh or dried
2 tablespoons vegetable oil
450 g (14 oz) lamb fillets, sliced into
    1 cm pieces
2 carrots, cut into ½ cm x 4 cm sticks
1 red capsicum (pepper), cut into strips
1 yellow capsicum, cut into strips
200 g (7 oz) bok choy (pak choi), sliced
200 g (7 oz) bean sprouts
4 spring onions (green onions),
    cut into thin strips

serves 4

i

preparation time
15 minutes

cooking time
12 minutes

**nutritional value
per serve**
fat: 3.4 g
carbohydrate: 12.9 g
protein: 7.8 g

1 In a bowl, combine the oyster and soy sauces, honey, lemon rind and juice. Mix well and set aside. Prepare the noodles according to the packet instructions.

2 Heat the wok until very hot. Add the oil and lamb and stir-fry for 5 minutes until seared on all sides. Add the carrots and capsicums and stir-fry for 4 minutes or until softened. Add the bok choy, bean sprouts and spring onions, and cook for a further 1 minute.

3 Reduce heat and add the noodles and the sauce mixture. Stir-fry for 2 minutes or until everything is hot and the lamb is cooked through.

beef and bean stir-fry

ingredients

2 teaspoons vegetable oil
2 cloves garlic, crushed
500 g (1 lb) topside or round steak,
   cut into thin strips across the grain
185 g (6 oz) snake (yard-long) or green
   beans, cut into 10 cm lengths
2 kaffir lime leaves, shredded
2 teaspoons brown sugar
2 tablespoons light soy sauce
1 tablespoon thai fish sauce
2 tablespoons fresh coriander
serves 4

i

preparation time
10 minutes

cooking time
6 minutes

**nutritional value
per serve**
fat: 4.4 g
carbohydrate: 1.8 g
protein: 14.5 g

1 Heat oil and garlic together in a wok over a medium heat. Increase heat to high. Add beef and stir-fry for 3 minutes or until beef changes colour.

2 Add beans, lime leaves, sugar and soy and fish sauces. Stir-fry for 2 minutes or until beans change colour. Stir in coriander and serve immediately.

korean marinated beef strips

ingredients

500 g (1 lb) lean beef fillet,
  sliced into 5 mm thick strips
2 spring onions (green onions),
  chopped
vegetable oil for brushing
chilli sauce to serve
extra spring onions to garnish

marinade

2 tablespoons sesame seeds
2 cloves garlic, finely chopped
2¹/₂ cm piece fresh root ginger,
  finely chopped
2 tablespoons sugar
3 tablespoons light soy sauce
3 tablespoons dark soy sauce
1 tablespoon sesame oil

serves 4

1 Heat a frying pan. Add the sesame seeds and dry-fry until golden, stirring constantly. Place in a small food processor or blender and grind finely. Add the garlic, ginger, sugar, light and dark soy sauces and oil and process or blend to a paste. In a non-metallic bowl, mix together the beef, spring onions and spice paste, turning to coat. Cover and marinate in the refrigerator for 4 hours.

i

preparation tme
20 minutes,
plus 4 hours
marinating

cooking time
10 minutes

**nutritional value
per serve**
fat: 8.1 g
carbohydrate: 5.3 g
protein: 15.8 g

2 Brush a ridged, cast-iron grill pan or large, heavy-based frying pan with the oil and heat until very hot. Add the beef strips in a single layer (you may have to cook them in batches) and cook for 1–2 minutes, turning once, until browned. Serve with chilli sauce, garnished with spring onions.

keema curry

ingredients

1 tablespoon vegetable oil
1 onion, finely chopped
2½ cm piece fresh root ginger, grated
2 cloves garlic, crushed
500 g (1 lb) lean minced lamb
2 teaspoons ground turmeric
1 teaspoon chilli powder
1 tablespoon garam masala
3 tablespoons tomato paste
450 ml (14 fl oz) lamb stock
125 g (4 oz) frozen peas
salt and black pepper
2 tablespoons chopped fresh coriander
extra coriander to garnish
serves 4

i

preparation time
10 minutes

cooking time
40-45 minutes

**nutritional value
per serve**
fat: 3 g
carbohydrate: 2.1 g
protein: 9.4 g

1 Heat the oil in a wok or large heavy-based frying pan. Add the onion, ginger and garlic and cook over a low heat for 5 minutes or until softened. Add minced lamb and stir to break up the mince with the back of a wooden spoon. Cook while stirring for 10 minutes or until the lamb browns.

2 Pour off any excess fat from the pan. Add the turmeric, chilli, garam masala and tomato paste, and stir-fry for 1–2 minutes. Add the stock and bring to the boil, stirring. Reduce the heat, cover and simmer for 15 minutes.

3 Add the peas and simmer for 10 minutes longer. Remove from the heat, stir in the salt, pepper and coriander. Garnish with coriander.

sizzling beef

ingredients

500 g (1 lb) rump steak,
  cut into thin strips
2 tablespoons soy sauce
2 tablespoons rice wine or sherry
1½ tablespoons cornflour
1 teaspoon sugar
3 tablespoons peanut oil
150 g (5 oz) broccoli,
  cut into bite-sized pieces
4 tablespoons water
1 large red capsicum (pepper),
  cut into thin strips
2 cloves garlic, crushed
3 tablespoons oyster sauce
200 g (7 oz) fresh bean sprouts
salt and black pepper

serves 4

i

preparation time
15 minutes

cooking time
20 minutes

**nutritional value
per serve**
fat: 6.8 g
carbohydrate: 4 g
protein: 10.4 g

1 Into a glass bowl, place the steak, soy sauce, rice wine or sherry, cornflour and sugar and mix thoroughly. Stand for 15 minutes. Heat the wok to a high heat. Add 1 tablespoon oil and one-third of the beef mixture and stir-fry for 2–3 minutes until browned. Remove and cook the remaining beef in 2 more batches, adding a little more oil if necessary.

2 Add the remaining oil and the broccoli. Slowly add the water and stir-fry for 5 minutes. Add the capsicum and garlic and stir-fry for a further 2–3 minutes. Stir in the oyster sauce.

3 Return the beef to the wok and add the bean sprouts. Toss over a high heat for 2 minutes or until the beef is reheated. Season to taste and serve immediately.

beef with green peppercorns

ingredients

500 g (1 lb) piece of topside
  or rump steak
2 teaspoons vegetable oil
2 cloves garlic, crushed
1 fresh green chilli, chopped
1 tablespoon green peppercorns in
  brine, drained and lightly crushed
1 green capsicum (pepper), chopped
3 tablespoons fresh coriander
$^1/_3$ cup (90 ml, 3 fl oz) coconut milk
2 teaspoons thai fish sauce
serves 4

1 Slice the steak into thin slices across the grain then cut each slice in half. Heat oil in a wok over a high heat. Add garlic and chilli and cook for 1 minute. Add beef and peppercorns and stir-fry in 2 batches for 3 minutes or until beef is browned.

2 Stir in capsicum, coriander, coconut milk and fish sauce and cook for 2 minutes longer.

preparation time
10 minutes

cooking time
10 minutes

**nutritional value
per serve**
fat: 7 g
carbohydrate: 1 g
protein: 15.5 g

honey beef with pineapple salsa

2 Heat 2 teaspoons oil in a wok over a medium heat. Add sesame seeds and garlic and stir-fry for 2 minutes or until seeds are golden. Remove seed mixture from wok with a slotted spoon and set aside.

3 Add remaining oil to wok. Add half the beef and stir-fry for 2 minutes or until brown, remove. Stir-fry the remaining beef adding extra oil if needed.

4 Add snow peas, zucchini, combined honey, soy and oyster sauces and sesame seed mixture. Stir-fry for 3 minutes or until sauce thickens. Remove to a platter. Serve immediately with pineapple salsa and steamed rice.

ingredients

1 tablespoon vegetable oil
2 tablespoons sesame seeds
2 cloves garlic, crushed
500 g (1 lb) lean beef strips
185 g (6 oz) snow peas (mangetout), trimmed
2 zucchini (courgettes), chopped
3 tablespoons honey
2 tablespoons soy sauce
1 tablespoon oyster sauce
steamed rice to serve

pineapple salsa

1/2 fresh pineapple, peeled, cored and diced
1 fresh red chilli, chopped
2 tablespoons brown sugar
2 tablespoons snipped fresh chives
2 tablespoons lime juice

serves 4

1 In a bowl, place the pineapple, chilli, sugar, chives and lime juice and toss to combine. Set aside.

i

preparation time
8 minutes

cooking time
8 minutes

nutritional value
per serve
fat: 4 g
carbohydrate: 9.6 g
protein: 8.8 g

country lamb

ingredients

1 tablespoon vegetable oil
1 onion, chopped
1 clove garlic, crushed
500 g (1 lb) lean lamb strips
1 carrot, sliced
2 zucchini (courgettes), sliced
125 g (4 oz) snow peas (mangetout)
125 g (4 oz) small button mushrooms
2 tablespoons chopped fresh parsley
freshly ground black pepper

red-wine sauce
1 cup (250 ml, 8 fl oz) lamb or beef stock
4 tablespoons red wine
1 tablespoon tomato paste
1 tablespoon worcestershire sauce
1 tablespoon cornflour
1 tablespoon water

serves 4-6

i

preparation time
15 minutes

cooking time
15 minutes

**nutritional value
per serve**
fat: 3.3 g
carbohydrate: 2.5 g
protein: 7.8 g

1 In a bowl, combine stock, wine, tomato paste and worcestershire sauce. Blend cornflour with water and stir into the mixture. Set aside.

2 Heat oil in a wok over a medium heat. Add onion and garlic and stir-fry for 3 minutes or until onion is golden. Increase heat to high, add lamb and stir-fry for 5 minutes or until lamb is brown. Remove lamb from wok and keep warm.

3 Add carrot, zucchini, snow peas and mushrooms to wok and stir-fry for 5 minutes or until vegetables are tender.

4 Return lamb to wok, stir in sauce mixture, bring to the boil and cook, stirring until sauce thickens slightly. Stir in parsley and season with black pepper. Serve immediately.

beef and broccoli curry

1 Heat oil in a wok over a medium heat. Add onion, garlic and ginger and stir-fry for 3 minutes or until onion is golden. Add curry paste and stir-fry for 2 minutes or until fragrant. Increase heat to high, add beef and stir-fry for 5 minutes or until brown.

2 Add broccoli and capsicum and stir-fry for 3 minutes or until vegetables are just tender. Stir in sugar, lime rind, coconut milk and fish sauce and simmer for 5 minutes or until sauce is heated. Scatter with peanuts and serve.

ingredients

1 tablespoon peanut oil
1 onion, chopped
2 cloves garlic, crushed
1 tablespoon finely grated fresh ginger
1 tablespoon red curry paste
500 g (1 lb) rump steak, trimmed and cut into thin strips
250 g (8 oz) broccoli, cut into small florets
1 red pepper (capsicum), chopped
1 tablespoon brown sugar
1 teaspoon finely grated lime rind (zest)
1½ cups (375 ml, 12 fl oz) coconut milk
1 tablespoon fish sauce
155 g (5 oz) unsalted peanuts, roasted
serves 4

i

preparation time
15 minutes

cooking time
14 minutes

nutritional value per serve
fat: 12.9 g
carbohydrate: 3.5 g
protein: 11.1 g

cashew and chilli beef curry

ingredients

3 cm piece fresh ginger, chopped
1 stalk fresh lemon grass, finely sliced
3 kaffir lime leaves, finely shredded
2 small fresh red chillies, deseeded and chopped
2 teaspoons shrimp paste
2 tablespoons thai fish sauce
1 tablespoon lime juice
2 tablespoons peanut oil
4 red or golden shallots, sliced
2 cloves garlic, chopped
3 small fresh red chillies, sliced
500 g (1 lb) round or blade steak, cut into 2 cm cubes
2 cups (500 ml, 16 fl oz) beef stock
125 g (4 oz) okra, trimmed
60 g (2 oz) cashew nuts, roughly chopped
1 tablespoon palm or brown sugar
2 tablespoons light soy sauce

serves 4-6

1 In a food processor, place ginger, lemon grass, lime leaves, chopped chillies, shrimp paste, fish sauce and lime juice and process to make a thick paste, adding a little water if necessary.

2 Heat 1 tablespoon oil in a wok over a medium heat. Add shallots, garlic, sliced chillies and spice paste and cook, stirring, for 2–3 minutes or until fragrant. Remove and set aside.

3 Wipe the wok clean and heat over a high heat. Add the remaining oil and the steak, in batches until brown. Return spice paste mixture to wok, stir in stock and okra and bring to the boil. Reduce heat, cover and simmer, stirring occasionally, for 25 minutes. Stir in cashews, sugar and soy sauce and simmer for 10 minutes longer or until beef is tender.

i

preparation time
15 minutes

cooking time
35-40 minutes

nutritional value per serve
fat: 6.1 g
carbohydrate: 2.5 g
protein: 9.5 g

red beef curry

ingredients

1 cup (250 ml, 8 fl oz) coconut cream
3 tablespoons thai red curry paste
500 g (1 lb) round or blade steak, cubed
155 g (5 oz) eggplant (aubergine), diced
220 g (7½ oz) can sliced bamboo shoots
6 kaffir lime leaves, crushed
1 tablespoon brown sugar
2 cups (500 ml, 16 fl oz) coconut milk
2 tablespoons thai fish sauce
3 tablespoons fresh coriander
2 fresh red chillies, chopped
jasmine steamed rice to serve
serves 4

i

preparation time
10 minutes
cooking time
48 minutes

**nutritional value
per serve**
fat: 11 g
carbohydrate: 3.1 g
protein: 7.3 g

1 Place coconut cream in a wok and bring to the boil over a high heat. Boil until oil separates from coconut cream and it reduces and thickens slightly. Stir in curry paste and boil for 2 minutes or until fragrant.

2 Add beef, eggplant, bamboo shoots, lime leaves, sugar, coconut milk and fish sauce. Cover and simmer for 40–45 minutes or until beef is tender. Stir in coriander and chillies. Serve over jasmine steamed rice.

vegetarian

1 Heat the oil in a wok, add the walnuts and stir-fry for 30 seconds. Add the onions and cook for a further 30 seconds.

2 Add the tomatoes, spinach and salt to taste. Cook for 1 minute or until the spinach begins to wilt, tossing to combine. Transfer the vegetables to a serving platter and sprinkle with the coriander to garnish. Serve immediately.

warm spinach salad with walnuts

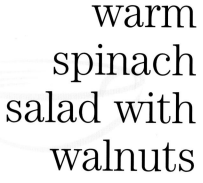

ingredients

1 tablespoon walnut oil
1 red onion, sliced into thin rings
5 sun-dried tomatoes in oil, drained and chopped
500 g (1 lb) baby spinach
3 tablespoons walnut pieces
salt
3 tablespoons chopped fresh coriander to garnish
serves 4

i

preparation time
5 minutes

cooking time
2 minutes

nutritional value per serve
fat: 6 g
carbohydrate: 2.2 g
protein: 2.9 g

snow peas and carrots with sesame seeds

ingredients

$1/2$ cucumber
2 tablespoons sesame seeds
1 tablespoon sunflower oil
4 carrots, cut into matchsticks
225 g ($7^1/2$ oz) snow peas (mangetout)
6 spring onions (green onions),
    chopped
1 tablespoon lemon juice
black pepper
serves 4

1 Peel the cucumber, cut it in half lengthways and scoop out the seeds. Slice into $1/2$ cm slices.

2 Heat a non-stick wok or large frying pan. Add the sesame seeds and dry-fry for 1 minute or until toasted, tossing constantly. Remove and set aside. Add the oil, then the cucumber and carrots and stir-fry over a high heat for 2 minutes.

3 Add the snow peas and spring onions and stir-fry for a further 2–3 minutes, until all the vegetables are cooked but still crisp. Sprinkle over the lemon juice and sesame seeds, toss to mix and stir-fry for a few seconds. Season with pepper and serve.

i

preparation time
10 minutes

cooking time
5 minutes

**nutritional value
per serve**
fat: 4.4 g
carbohydrate: 4.3 g
protein: 2.2 g

spinach with sesame seeds

ingredients

750 g (1½ lb) fresh silverbeet (spinach), stalks removed
1 tablespoon peanut oil
1 teaspoon sesame oil
3 cloves garlic, sliced
2 tablespoons sesame seeds
juice of ½ lemon
¼ teaspoon lemon rind (zest), finely grated
salt and black pepper

serves 6

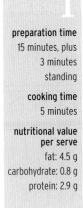

i

preparation time
15 minutes, plus
3 minutes
standing

cooking time
5 minutes

nutritional value per serve
fat: 4.5 g
carbohydrate: 0.8 g
protein: 2.9 g

1 In a large bowl, place the silverbeet, cover with boiling water, and leave for 2–3 minutes. Drain, then refresh under cold running water. Squeeze out any excess water, then coarsely chop.

2 Heat the peanut and sesame oil in a wok or large, heavy-based frying pan. Add the garlic and the sesame seeds and fry for 1–2 minutes, until the garlic has begun to brown and the seeds have started to pop. Stir in the spinach and fry for 1–2 minutes, until heated through. Add the lemon juice, lemon rind, salt and pepper and mix well. Place on a serving platter and serve immediately.

wilted rocket cheese salad

ingredients

3 tablespoons olive oil

4 slices white bread, crusts removed and cut into cubes

3 spring onions (green onions), sliced diagonally

2 cloves garlic, crushed

2 zucchini (courgettes), cut lengthwise into thin strips

1 red capsicum (pepper), thinly sliced

90 g (3 oz) raisins

2 bunches (about 250 g, 8 oz) rocket

125 g (4 oz) blue cheese, crumbled

2 tablespoons balsamic vinegar

serves 4

1 Heat 2 tablespoons oil in a wok over a medium heat. Add bread cubes and stir-fry for 3 minutes or until golden.

Drain on absorbent kitchen paper. Heat remaining oil in wok, add spring onions and garlic and stir-fry for 2 minutes. Add zucchini, capsicum and raisins and stir-fry for 3 minutes or until vegetables are just tender. Remove from wok and set aside.

2 Add rocket to the wok and stir-fry for 2 minutes or until rocket just wilts. Place rocket on a serving platter or divide between individual bowls or plates, top with vegetable mixture and scatter with croutons and blue cheese. Drizzle with balsamic vinegar and serve immediately.

i

preparation time
10 minutes

cooking time
10 minutes

nutritional value per serve
fat: 10.1 g
carbohydrate: 12.3 g
protein: 4.7 g

eggplant and bean with basil

ingredients

3 eggplants (aubergines), halved lengthways and cut into ¹/₂ cm thick slices

salt

1 tablespoon vegetable oil

2 onions, cut into thin wedges, layers separated

3 fresh red chillies, chopped

2 cloves garlic, sliced

1 stalk fresh lemon grass, chopped

250 g (8 oz) green beans, trimmed

1 cup (250 ml, 8 fl oz) coconut milk

45 g (1¹/₂ oz) basil leaves

serves 6

i

preparation time
5 minutes, plus 20 minutes resting

cooking time
18 minutes

nutritional value per serve
fat: 4.9 g
carbohydrate: 3.2 g
protein: 1.5 g

1 Place eggplants in a colander, sprinkle with salt and set aside for 20 minutes. Rinse under cold running water and pat dry on absorbent kitchen paper.

2 Heat oil in a wok or frying pan over a high heat. Add onions, chillies, garlic and lemon grass and stir-fry for 3 minutes. Add eggplants, beans and coconut milk and heat until almost boiling. Turn down heat, cover and simmer for 15 minutes until eggplants are tender. Stir in basil and serve immediately.

stir-fried bitter melon

ingredients

1 medium bitter melon (gourd), peeled,
    seeds removed, cut into 1 cm
      thick slices
2 tablespoons salt
1 teaspoon vegetable oil
3 tablespoons small dried prawns
6 red or golden shallots, sliced
2 cloves garlic, sliced
2 stalks fresh lemon grass, finely sliced
3 fresh green chillies, finely sliced
1 small red pawpaw (papaya), cut
    into 3 cm cubes
125 g (4 oz) snow peas (mangetout),
    halved
1 tablespoon tamarind concentrate
serves 4

i

preparation time
5 minutes, plus
30 minutes
resting

cooking time
10 minutes

**nutritional value
per serve**
fat: 0.6 g
carbohydrate: 5.7 g
protein: 2.1 g

1 Rub each slice of bitter melon with salt, place in a colander and set aside for 30 minutes. Rinse under cold water and drain thoroughly.

2 Heat oil in a wok over a medium heat. Add dried prawns, shallots, garlic and lemon grass and stir-fry for 4 minutes or until shallots are golden.

3 Add chillies and bitter melon and stir-fry for 4 minutes or until melon is tender. Add pawpaw, snow peas and tamarind and stir-fry for 2 minutes or until snow peas are tender.

sweet potato and tofu curry

ingredients

1 tablespoon peanut oil
1 teaspoon chilli oil (optional)
315 g (10 oz) firm tofu, cut into 1 cm
    thick slices
1¹/₂ cups (375 ml, 12 fl oz) coconut cream
1 cup (250 ml, 8 fl oz) vegetable stock
2 teaspoons thai red curry paste
375 g (12 oz) orange sweet potato,
    cut into 2 cm cubes
2 teaspoons palm or brown sugar
1 tablespoon thai fish sauce or light
    soy sauce
2 teaspoons lime juice
60 g (2 oz) fresh basil leaves

serves 4

1 Heat peanut oil and chilli oil, if using, in a wok over a medium heat. Add tofu in 2 batches and stir-fry until brown on all sides. Remove, drain on absorbent kitchen paper and set aside.

2 Wipe wok clean with kitchen paper, then add coconut cream and stock and bring to the boil. Stir in curry paste and cook for 3–4 minutes or until fragrant. Add sweet potato, cover and cook over a medium heat for 8–10 minutes or until sweet potato is almost cooked.

3 Stir in sugar, fish sauce and lime juice and cook for 3 minutes.

4 Return tofu to the wok and simmer 2 minutes to heat. Stir in basil leaves.

i

preparation time
15 minutes

cooking time
30 minutes

**nutritional value
per serve**
fat: 8.4 g
carbohydrate: 5.6 g
protein: 3.9 g

red bean stir-fry

ingredients

185 g (6 oz) fettuccine
1 tablespoon vegetable oil
1 onion, chopped
2 cloves garlic, crushed
250 g (8 oz) asparagus, cut into
   5 cm lengths
125 g (4 oz) green beans
125 g (4 oz) snow peas (mangetout)
440 g (14 oz) can red kidney beans,
   drained and rinsed
250 g (8 oz) tomato salsa
2 tablespoons chopped fresh coriander
90 g (3 oz) pine nuts, toasted
serves 4

i

preparation time
15 minutes

cooking time
25 minutes

**nutritional value
per serve**
fat: 5.8 g
carbohydrate: 7.8 g
protein: 2.6 g

1 Cook fettuccine in boiling water in a large saucepan until al dente. Drain well and set aside to cool slightly.

2 Heat oil in a wok over a medium heat. Add onion and garlic and stir-fry for 3 minutes or until onion is golden. Add asparagus, beans and snow peas and stir-fry for 3 minutes or until vegetables are just tender. Add red kidney beans, tomato salsa and coriander and stir-fry for 5 minutes.

3 Add fettuccine, toss to combine and cook for 3 minutes or until heated through. Scatter with pine nuts and serve immediately.

vegetarian hokkien noodles

ingredients

500 g (1 lb) fresh hokkien noodles
2 teaspoons vegetable oil
2 cloves garlic, crushed
2 teaspoons finely grated fresh ginger
2 fresh red chillies, chopped
1 bunch (about 500 g, 1 lb) bok choy
  (pak choi), chopped
220 g (7^1/$_2$ oz) can bamboo shoots, sliced
1 red capsicum (pepper), chopped
6 spring onions (green onions),
  chopped
155 g (5 oz) oyster mushrooms
60 g (2 oz) bean sprouts
1^1/$_2$ tablespoons soy sauce
1^1/$_2$ tablespoons hoisin sauce
1 tablespoon oyster sauce
1 tablespoon sweet chilli sauce
serves 4

1 Cook noodles in boiling water in a large saucepan for 3 minutes or until tender. Drain, rinse under cold water, drain again and set aside.

2 Heat oil in a wok over a medium heat. Add garlic, ginger and chillies and stir-fry for 2 minutes or until golden. Add bok choy, bamboo shoots, capsicum, spring onions and noodles and stir-fry for 3 minutes.

3 Add mushrooms and beans sprouts. In a bowl, combine soy, hoisin, oyster and chilli sauces. Stir combined sauces into the wok and stir-fry for 4 minutes or until heated through.

i

preparation time
10 minutes

cooking time
12 minutes

nutritional value per serve
fat: 1.1 g
carbohydrate: 17.3g
protein: 4.1 g

stir-fried vegetables

ingredients

2 tablespoons vegetable or peanut oil
5 cm piece fresh root ginger, peeled and finely chopped
3 cloves garlic, finely chopped
2 tablespoons dry sherry
1 red capsicum (pepper), cut into 2.5 cm squares
1 yellow capsicum, cut into 2.5 cm squares
2 medium carrots, peeled and thinly sliced on the diagonal
350 g (11½ oz) broccoli, cut into small florets and stalks thinly sliced
300 g (10 oz) brown cap mushrooms, wiped and thickly sliced
2 tablespoons soy sauce
8 spring onions (green onions), cut into 1 cm diagonal slices

serves 4

1 Prepare and cut all vegetables. Measure liquid ingredients and place in small bowls. Arrange all in order of inclusion.

2 Heat a large wok over a high heat for 1 minute. Add the oil and rotate the wok to coat the base and lower sides. Add the ginger and garlic and stir-fry for 30 seconds. Add the sherry and cook for a further 15 seconds. Add the capsicums and carrots and continue to stir-fry for 5 minutes or until the vegetables start to soften.

3 Add the broccoli, mushrooms and soy sauce and stir-fry for 3 minutes or until all the vegetables are just tender. Add the spring onions and stir-fry for 1 minute. Serve immediately.

i

preparation time
25 minutes

cooking time
11 minutes

nutritional value per serve
fat: 3.3 g
carbohydrate: 2.4 g
protein: 3.0 g

warm vegetable salad

ingredients

1 tablespoon vegetable oil
125 g (4 oz) blanched hazelnuts
2 onions, chopped
2 carrots, sliced
2 zucchini (courgettes), chopped
155 g (5 oz) snow peas (mangetout)
4 field mushrooms, sliced
1 green capsicum (pepper), sliced
1 red capsicum, sliced
6 spring onions (green onions), chopped
250 g (8 oz) asparagus, halved
red wine and thyme vinaigrette
⅓ cup (90 ml, 3 fl oz) olive oil
4 tablespoons red-wine vinegar
1 tablespoon chopped fresh thyme
1 teaspoon sugar
freshly ground black pepper
serves 4

preparation time
10 minutes

cooking time
12 minutes

nutritional value per serve
fat: 11 g
carbohydrate: 3.5 g
protein: 2.6 g

1 In a screw-top jar, place olive oil, vinegar, thyme, sugar and black pepper and shake well to combine. Set aside. Heat 2 teaspoons vegetable oil in a wok over a high heat. Add hazelnuts and stir-fry for 3 minutes. Set aside.

2 Heat remaining oil in the wok. Add onions and stir-fry for 3 minutes or until golden. Add carrots, zucchini, snow peas, mushrooms, capsicums, spring onions and asparagus and stir-fry for 5 minutes. Return hazelnuts to wok, add vinaigrette and toss to combine.

chicken

lime-glazed chicken wings

ingredients

1 kg (2 lb) chicken wings, tips removed
4 tablespoons lime juice
1 tablespoon white-wine vinegar
2 tablespoons brown sugar
2 teaspoons soy sauce
2 tablespoons oil
4 spring onions (green onions),
  diagonally sliced
2 limes, thinly sliced
1/2 cup (125 ml, 4 fl oz) water
4 tablespoons white sugar
1/2 teaspoon white-wine vinegar
makes 12

i

preparation time
10 minutes,
plus 30 minutes
marinating

cooking time
18 minutes

**nutritional value
per serve**
fat: 5.5 g
carbohydrate: 6.2 g
protein: 13.7 g

1 Place chicken wings in a flat non-metal container. In a bowl, combine lime juice, vinegar, sugar and soy sauce. Pour over the wings and turn to coat. Marinate for 30 minutes or longer.

2 Heat the wok and add oil. Remove wings from marinade and stir-fry about 15 minutes until brown and tender. Add spring onions and stir-fry 1 minute. Pour in the marinade. Stir to coat and heat through. Remove to a platter and keep hot.

3 Add the lime and water to the wok and simmer 2 minutes. Stir in the sugar and vinegar, and cook until slices are coated with a thick syrup. Arrange slices over the wings. Pour over remaining syrup. Serve as finger food or as a meal with rice and vegetables.

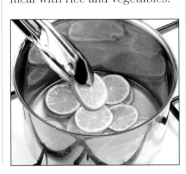

sweet and sour chicken

ingredients

1 x 420 g (14 oz) can pineapple pieces
2 teaspoons soy sauce
2 tablespoons malt vinegar
2 tablespoons brown sugar
1 tablespoon lemon juice
1 teaspoon finely grated fresh ginger
2 tablespoons tomato sauce
3 tablespoons oil
500 g (1 lb) chicken thigh fillets,
   cut into 1 cm wide strips
1 tablespoon cornflour
2 tablespoons water
1 red capsicum (pepper), deseeded
   and cut into squares
6 spring onions (green onions),
   diagonally sliced
boiled rice to serve

serves 6

1 Drain pineapple pieces and reserve the juice. In a bowl, mix together the pineapple juice, soy sauce, vinegar, sugar, lemon juice, ginger and tomato sauce. Set aside.

2 Heat the wok on high heat. Add 2 tablespoons of oil, and ⅓ of the chicken. Stir-fry over high heat for about 1 minute until cooked. Remove and cook remaining chicken in 2 batches, adding extra oil if needed. Drain chicken well on absorbent paper. Drain all oil from the wok.

3 In a cup, blend the cornflour with the water. Pour the sauce mixture into the wok and add the blended cornflour. Cook stirring until mixture boils and thickens. Stir in capsicum, spring onions and pineapple pieces, and cook 1 minute. Add chicken and heat through. Serve immediately with boiled rice.

i

preparation time
10 minutes

cooking time
8 minutes

nutritional value per serve
fat: 5.5 g
carbohydrate: 16 g
protein: 6.2 g

chicken rolls with apricot dipping sauce

ingredients

2 tablespoons oil
1 clove garlic, finely chopped
2 teaspoons finely chopped fresh ginger
1 small onion, finely chopped
500 g (1 lb) chicken breast or stir-fry pieces, finely chopped
1/4 chinese cabbage, finely chopped
1 red capsicum (pepper), deseeded and thinly sliced
6 mushrooms, thinly sliced
4 water chestnuts, chopped
1 tablespoon soy sauce
1 tablespoon oyster sauce
2 teaspoons cornflour
1 tablespoon water
1 packet spring roll wrappers
1 egg white, lightly beaten
oil for deep frying

dipping sauce
160 g (5 1/2 oz) apricot jam
1 tablespoon soy sauce
1 tablespoon lemon juice
2 tablespoons white vinegar
1 tablespoon water

makes 16

1 Heat the wok on high heat. Add 2 tablespoons of oil, garlic, ginger and onion and stir-fry for 1 minute. Add chicken and stir-fry for 2 minutes.

2 Add the cabbage, capsicum, mushrooms and water chestnuts. Stir-fry for 2 minutes. In a cup, blend the cornflour. Push the mixture in the wok to the sides, and pour soy and oyster sauce and blended cornflour in the centre. Stir until sauce thickens then toss through the chicken mixture. Spread mixture onto a flat tray to cool.

3 Place a heaped tablespoon of mixture along one end of wrapper 2 cm from front and side edges. Brush edges with egg white. Roll up, folding in the sides.

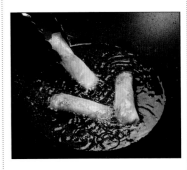

4 Heat a clean wok, add oil to approximately 5 cm deep and heat. Fry the rolls a few at a time until golden. Drain on paper towel.

5 In a saucepan, mix together the apricot jam, soy sauce, lemon juice, vinegar and water. Heat gently while stirring. Serve hot spring rolls with the dipping sauce.

i

preparation time
10 minutes

cooking time
20 minutes

nutritional value per serve
fat: 13.7 g
carbohydrate: 15.7 g
protein: 8.6 g

fried noodles with chicken stir-fry

ingredients

200 g (7 oz) fresh wheat noodles
250 g (8 oz) chicken breast fillets
$1/2$ teaspoon salt
$1/2$ teaspoon five-spice powder
2 tablespoons oil
1 clove garlic, chopped
1 red capsicum (pepper), deseeded and
    cut into strips or squares
4 mushrooms, sliced
4 spring onions (green onions)
2 baby bok choy (pak choi), leaves
    separated
425 g (14 oz) can baby corn, drained
1 tablespoon dry sherry
2 teaspoons cornflour
1 tablespoon oyster sauce
serves 4-6

preparation time
10 minutes

cooking time
8 minutes

**nutritional value
per serve**
fat: 4.8 g
carbohydrate: 17.8 g
protein: 8.3 g

1 Soak noodles in hot water for 5 minutes and drain. Cut chicken breasts into 2 cm wide strips and sprinkle with salt and five-spice powder. Set aside. Heat wok, add 1 tablespoon oil and rotate wok to coat lower sides. Add noodles and stir-fry for 2 minutes until golden. Remove and keep hot.

2 Add 2 teaspoons oil, garlic and chicken and stir-fry for 2 minutes. Add the capsicum, mushrooms, spring onions, bok choy and corn and continue to stir-fry 2–3 minutes. Mix the sherry and cornflour together, add the oyster sauce and drizzle over the ingredients. Toss through for 1 minute to heat and thicken the juices. Pile over the noodles and serve immediately.

samosas

ingredients

1 tablespoon vegetable oil
2 medium onions, finely chopped
1 clove garlic, crushed
2 teaspoons curry paste
$\frac{1}{2}$ teaspoon salt
1 tablespoon white vinegar
250 g (8 oz) chicken mince
$\frac{1}{2}$ cup (125 ml, 4 fl oz) water
2 teaspoons sweet chilli sauce
2 tablespoons chopped coriander
1 packet spring roll wrappers
oil for deep frying
makes 30

preparation time
15 minutes

cooking time
30 minutes

nutritional value per serve
fat: 25.2 g
carbohydrate: 12.6 g
protein: 5.9 g

1 Heat the wok, add oil and fry onions and garlic until soft. Stir in curry paste, salt and vinegar. Add chicken mince and stir-fry on high until it changes colour. Reduce the heat. Add the water, cover and cook about 6 minutes until most of the water is absorbed. Add sweet chilli sauce and coriander, stir to mix well. Remove to a plate to cool.

2 Cut 10 spring roll wrappers into 3 even pieces lengthwise. Place a teaspoon of filling at the end and fold the pastry over diagonally, forming a triangle. Fold again on the straight; and continue to end of strip. Moisten the inside edge of the last fold with water and press gently to seal.

3 Heat clean wok. Add enough oil to be approximately 5 cm deep and heat. Add 3–4 samosas at a time and fry until golden. Remove to a tray lined with paper towels. Serve hot.

stir-fry chicken with almonds and broccoli

ingredients

200 g (7 oz) broccoli florets
500 g (1 lb) chicken stir-fry pieces
3 teaspoons cornflour
$1/2$ teaspoon five-spice powder
$1/2$ teaspoon salt
oil for frying
150 g (5 oz) blanched almonds
$1^1/2$ teaspoons finely chopped
   fresh ginger
1 clove garlic, crushed
2 tablespoons dry sherry
1 teaspoon sugar
1 tablespoon soy sauce
2 teaspoons water
2 teaspoons cornflour
boiled rice to serve
serves 4

1 Place broccoli florets in boiling water for 1 minute then remove to a bowl of iced water, stand 5 minutes, drain and set aside. In a bowl, place the chicken and sprinkle with cornflour, five-spice powder and salt. Mix well and set aside.

2 Heat 2 tablespoons oil in the wok and fry the almonds until golden. Remove, drain and set aside. Add the ginger and garlic and stir-fry for 1 minute. Add the chicken in batches and stir-fry until the chicken is cooked.

3 Return all the chicken to the wok and add the sherry, sugar and soy sauce. Stir a little then add the combined water and cornflour. Stir-fry until the sauce thickens. Add the blanched broccoli and fried almonds and toss to heat through. Serve immediately with boiled rice.

i

preparation time
15 minutes

cooking time
10 minutes

**nutritional value
per serve**
fat: 9.7 g
carbohydrate: 13.4 g
protein: 10.4 g

stir-fried lemon grass chicken

ingredients

2 stalks lemon grass

500 g (1 lb) chicken breast fillets, cut into 2.5cm cubes

1 teaspoon sesame oil

2 tablespoons vegetable oil

½ red capsicum (pepper), deseeded and chopped

2 tablespoons roasted salted peanuts, roughly chopped

2 tablespoons thai fish sauce

1 teaspoon sugar

salt

2 spring onions (green onions), chopped

serves 4

i

preparation time
10 minutes, plus 2 hours or overnight marinating

cooking time
10 minutes

nutritional value per serve
fat: 13 g
carbohydrate: 3.9 g
protein: 16.8 g

1 Finely chop the lower white bulbous parts of the lemon grass. In a large bowl, place the chicken, lemon grass and sesame oil and turn to coat. Cover and marinate in the refrigerator for 2 hours or overnight.

2 Heat a wok or large, heavy-based frying pan. Add the vegetable oil. Add the chicken with its marinade and stir-fry for 5 minutes or until the chicken has turned white. Add the capsicum, peanuts, fish sauce, sugar and salt. Stir-fry for another 5 minutes or until the chicken and capsicum are cooked. Sprinkle over the spring onions just before serving.

provençal chicken

ingredients

1 tablespoon vegetable oil
1 red onion, chopped
2 cloves garlic, crushed
2 tablespoons capers, drained
   and chopped
4 boneless chicken thighs, chopped
440 g (14 oz) can cannellini beans
200 g (7 oz) marinated artichoke hearts
125 g (4 oz) kalamata olives, pitted
375 ml (12 fl oz) tomato pasta sauce
2 tablespoons chopped fresh parsley
freshly ground black pepper
serves 4

i

preparation time
10 minutes

cooking time
21-23 minutes

**nutritional value
per serve**
fat: 5 g
carbohydrate: 5.9 g
protein: 9.6 g

1 Heat oil in a wok over a medium heat. Add onion, garlic and capers and stir-fry for 3 minutes or until onion is golden. Add chicken and stir-fry for 5 minutes or until chicken is brown.

2 Add beans, artichokes and olives and stir-fry for 3 minutes. Stir in pasta sauce and parsley and cook, stirring frequently, for 10 minutes or until sauce thickens slightly. Season to taste with black pepper.

garlic pepper chicken

ingredients

2 teaspoons vegetable oil
4 cloves garlic, crushed
1 teaspoon black peppercorns, crushed
4 chicken breast fillets, sliced
½ cup (125 ml, 4 fl oz) chicken stock
4 tablespoons dry white wine
1 tablespoon soy sauce
155 g (5 oz) young english spinach leaves
serves 4

i

preparation time
5 minutes

cooking time
8 minutes

**nutritional value
per serve**
fat: 4.8 g
carbohydrate: 1.9 g
protein: 17 g

1 Heat oil in a wok over a medium heat. Add garlic and black peppercorns and stir-fry for 1 minute or until garlic is golden. Add chicken and stir-fry for 3 minutes or until brown.

2 Stir in stock, wine and soy sauce. Bring to simmering and simmer for 4 minutes or until sauce reduces by half.

3 Arrange spinach leaves on serving plates and top with chicken mixture. Serve immediately.

chicken salad with mint dressing

ingredients

1 teaspoon sesame oil
1 teaspoon chilli oil
1 stalk fresh lemon grass,
   finely chopped
315 g (10 oz) lean chicken mince
185 g (6 oz) water chestnuts, chopped
1 tablespoon soy sauce
200 g (7 oz) assorted lettuce leaves
1 red capsicum (pepper), thinly sliced
1 green capsicum, thinly sliced
60 g (2 oz) bean sprouts
45 g (1¹/₂ oz) shredded coconut, toasted

mint dressing

3 tablespoons chopped fresh mint
1 clove garlic, crushed
1 tablespoon brown sugar
4 tablespoons water
1 tablespoon fish sauce
1 tablespoon lime juice

serves 4

i

preparation time
5 minutes

cooking time
8 minutes

**nutritional value
per serve**
fat: 4.1 g
carbohydrate: 3.9 g
protein: 6.5 g

1 In a bowl, place the mint, garlic, sugar, water, fish sauce and lime juice and mix to combine. Set aside. Heat sesame and chilli oils in a wok over a medium heat. Add the lemon grass and stir-fry for 2 minutes or until golden. Add the chicken, water chestnuts and soy sauce and stir-fry for 5 minutes or until chicken is tender. Remove pan from heat and cool slightly.

2 In a bowl, place the chicken mixture, capsicums, bean sprouts and coconut and toss to combine. On a large platter, place the lettuce leaves and arrange over the chicken mixture.

seafood

cashew and prawn egg-fried rice

ingredients

350 g (11½ oz) long-grain rice
450 ml (14 fl oz) water
salt
2 tablespoons peanut oil
1 clove garlic, finely chopped
1 cm piece fresh root ginger,
    finely chopped
2 spring onions (green onions), sliced
    diagonally, white and green parts
    separated
60 g (2 oz) roasted salted cashew nuts,
    chopped
75 g (2½ oz) baby sweetcorn, cut into
    1 cm lengths
200 g (7 oz) cooked peeled tiger prawns
2 tablespoons medium-dry sherry
3 tablespoons light soy sauce
2 teaspoons sesame oil
1 large egg, beaten
black pepper
serves 4

1 Rinse the rice, then place it in a large saucepan with water and salt. Bring to the boil, reduce the heat and simmer for 15 minutes or until tender. Rinse with cold water and drain well. Spread on a

tray and leave to cool for 40–60 minutes, fluffing it up occasionally with a fork.

2 Heat a wok or large frying pan and add the oil. Add the garlic, ginger and white parts of the spring onions and stir-fry for 1–2 minutes. Mix in the rice and stir-fry for 2 minutes, tossing quickly and high. Add the cashew nuts and sweetcorn and stir-fry for 2 minutes. Add the prawns and sherry and stir-fry for 1 minute. Pour over the soy sauce and sesame oil and cook for a further 2 minutes, stirring.

3 Drizzle over the egg and stir-fry for 2–3 minutes, until cooked through. Season with black pepper and sprinkle over the green parts of the spring onions. Serve immediately.

i

preparation time
15 minutes,
plus 40-60
minutes cooling

cooking time
25 minutes

**nutritional value
per serve**
fat: 6.6 g
carbohydrate: 22 g
protein: 8.1 g

goan-style fish and coconut curry

ingredients

2 tomatoes
2 cardamom pods, husks discarded
  and seeds reserved
1 teaspoon ground coriander
1 teaspoon ground cumin
1 teaspoon ground cinnamon
1 teaspoon chilli powder
½ teaspoon ground turmeric
2 tablespoons vegetable oil
1 onion, finely chopped
1 clove garlic, finely chopped
2.5 cm piece fresh root ginger,
  finely chopped
400 ml (13 fl oz) coconut milk
fish fillet, such as haddock or cod,
  cut into 2.5 cm chunks
salt
steamed rice to serve
fresh coriander to garnish
serves 4

preparation time
15 minutes, plus
40-60 minutes
cooling

cooking time
25 minutes

**nutritional value
per serve**
fat: 7.3 g
carbohydrate: 13.3 g
protein: 3.5 g

1 In a bowl, place the tomatoes and cover with boiling water. Leave to stand for 30 seconds. Skin and deseed the tomatoes, then dice. Crush the cardamom seeds using a mortar and pestle. To the mortar, add the coriander, cumin, cinnamon, chilli powder, turmeric and 2 tablespoons of water and mix to a paste. Set aside.

2 Heat a large wok. Add the oil and fry the onion, garlic and ginger for 3 minutes or until softened. Add the spice paste, mix well and fry for 1 minute, stirring constantly.

3 Pour in the coconut milk and bring to the boil, stirring. Reduce the heat and simmer for 10 minutes or until the liquid has reduced slightly. Add the fish, tomatoes and salt to taste. Partly cover the wok and simmer for a further 10 minutes or until the fish turns opaque and is cooked through, stirring occasionally. Serve with steamed rice and garnish with coriander.

coconut prawns and scallops

ingredients

1 kg (2 lb) large green prawns, shelled
    and deveined, tails left intact
3 egg whites, lightly beaten
90 g (3 oz) shredded coconut
vegetable oil for deep-frying
1 tablespoon peanut oil
4 fresh red chillies, deseeded and sliced
2 small fresh green chillies, deseeded
    and sliced
2 cloves garlic, crushed
1 tablespoon shredded fresh ginger
3 kaffir lime leaves, finely shredded
375 g (12 oz) scallops
125 g (4 oz) snow pea (mangetout)
    sprouts or leaves
2 tablespoons palm or brown sugar
4 tablespoons lime juice
2 tablespoons thai fish sauce
1 lime for garnish
serves 6

1 Dip prawns into the beaten egg white, then press into the shredded coconut to coat both sides. Place in single layer on a flat tray, cover and refrigerate 30 minutes.

2 Heat a large wok and add enough oil to be at least 5 cm deep. Add prawns, a few at a time and cook for 2–3 minutes or until golden and crisp. Drain on absorbent kitchen paper and keep warm. Drain oil from wok.

3 Reheat the wok over a high heat. Add peanut oil, chillies, garlic, ginger and lime leaves and stir-fry for 2–3 minutes or until fragrant. Add scallops to wok and stir-fry for 3 minutes or until opaque.

4 Add snow pea sprouts or leaves, sugar, lime juice and fish sauce and stir-fry for 2 minutes or until heated. Divide between serving bowls and top each with cooked prawns. Garnish with lime twists or quarters.

i

preparation time
15 minutes,
plus 30 minutes
refrigeration

cooking time
10 minutes

**nutritional value
per serve**
fat: 7.3 g
carbohydrate: 2.7 g
protein: 13.9 g

stir-fried tamarind prawns

ingredients

2 tablespoons tamarind pulp

½ cup (125 ml, 4 fl oz) water

2 teaspoons vegetable oil

3 stalks fresh lemon grass, chopped, or 2 teaspoons finely grated lemon rind (zest)

2 fresh red chillies, chopped

500 g (1 lb) medium green prawns, shelled and deveined, tails intact

2 green (unripe) mangoes, peeled and thinly sliced

3 tablespoons chopped fresh coriander leaves

2 tablespoons brown sugar

2 tablespoons lime juice

serves 4

i

preparation time
20 minutes, plus 20 minutes standing

cooking time
10 minutes

nutritional value per serve
fat: 2.3 g
carbohydrate: 6.9 g
protein: 9.8 g

1 In a bowl, place tamarind pulp and water and stand for 20 minutes. Strain, reserve liquid and set aside. Discard solids. Heat oil in a wok or frying pan over a high heat. Add lemon grass or lemon rind and chillies and stir-fry for 1 minute. Add prawns and stir-fry for 2 minutes or until they change colour.

2 Add mangoes, coriander, sugar, lime juice and tamarind liquid and stir-fry for 5 minutes or until prawns are cooked.

pad thai with pork and prawns

ingredients

250 g (8 oz) rice noodles
4 tablespoons peanut oil
2 cloves garlic, chopped
1 shallot, chopped
125 g (4 oz) pork fillet, cut into 5mm
 thick strips
1 tablespoon thai fish sauce
1 teaspoon sugar
juice of $1/2$ lime
1 tablespoon light soy sauce
1 tablespoon tomato sauce
200 g (7 oz) fresh bean sprouts
125 g (4 oz) cooked and peeled prawns
black pepper
60 g (2 oz) roasted salted peanuts,
 chopped
1 tablespoon chopped fresh coriander
1 lime, quartered, to serve
serves 4

i

preparation time
20 minutes

cooking time
15 minutes

**nutritional value
per serve**
fat: 10.6 g
carbohydrate: 7.1 g
protein: 8 g

1 Prepare the rice noodles according to the packet instructions, rinse and drain well. Heat a wok. Add the oil, garlic, shallot and pork and stir-fry for 3 minutes or until the pork turns opaque. Stir in the rice noodles and mix thoroughly.

2 In a bowl, mix together the fish sauce, sugar, lime juice, soy sauce and tomato sauce.

Add sauce mixture to the wok, stirring well. Stir-fry for 5 minutes. Mix in the bean sprouts and prawns and stir-fry for a further 5 minutes or until the bean sprouts are tender. Season with black pepper.

3 Transfer to a serving dish. Sprinkle over the peanuts and coriander, then serve with the lime wedges.

sichuan-style scallops

ingredients

1½ tablespoons peanut oil
1 tablespoon finely chopped ginger
1 tablespoon finely chopped garlic
2 tablespoons finely chopped spring
   onions (green onions)
500 g (1 lb) scallops, including corals
steamed rice to serve

mint dressing

1 tablespoon rice wine or dry sherry
2 teaspoons light soy sauce
2 teaspoons dark soy sauce
2 tablespoons chilli bean sauce
2 teaspoons tomato paste
1 teaspoon sugar
2 teaspoons sesame oil

serves 4

preparation time
8 minutes

cooking time
5 minutes

**nutritional value
per serve**
fat: 3.2 g
carbohydrate: 15.6 g
protein: 5.7 g

1 Heat wok until very hot. Add the oil and when it is very hot add the ginger, garlic and spring onions. Stir-fry for 10 seconds. Add the scallops and stir-fry for 1 minute.

2 In a bowl, combine the rice wine or sherry, soy sauces, chilli bean sauce, tomato paste and sugar. Add to the scallops. Stir-fry for 4 minutes until the scallops are firm and thoroughly coated with the sauce.

3 Add the sesame oil and stir-fry for 1 minute. Serve at once with steamed rice.

deep-fried chilli fish

ingredients

2 x 500 g (1 lb) whole fish such as
   bream, snapper, whiting, sea perch,
   cod or haddock, scaled and gutted
4 red chillies, chopped
4 fresh coriander roots
3 cloves garlic, crushed
1 teaspoon black peppercorns, crushed
vegetable oil for deep-frying
red chilli sauce
$^2/_3$ cup (170 g, $5^1/_2$ oz) sugar
8 fresh red chillies, sliced
4 red or golden shallots, sliced
$^1/_3$ cup (90 ml, 3 fl oz) coconut vinegar
$^1/_3$ cup (90 ml, 3 fl oz) water
serves 2-4

1 Make diagonal slashes along both sides of the fish. In a food processor, place chopped chillies, coriander roots, garlic and black peppercorns and process to make a paste. Spread mixture over both sides of fish and marinate for 30 minutes.

2 In a saucepan, place the sugar, sliced chillies, shallots, vinegar and water. Cook, stirring, over a low heat until sugar dissolves. Bring mixture to simmering and simmer, stirring occasionally, for 4 minutes or until sauce thickens.

3 Heat vegetable oil in a wok or deep-frying pan until a cube of bread dropped in browns in 50 seconds. Cook fish, one at a time, for 2 minutes each side or until crisp and flesh flakes when tested with a fork. Drain on absorbent kitchen paper. Serve with chilli sauce.

i

preparation time
8 minutes, plus
30 minutes
marinating

cooking time
14 minutes

**nutritional value
per serve**
fat: 3.9 g
carbohydrate: 11 g
protein: 13.7 g

scallops with zucchini in apple butter

ingredients

2 zucchini (courgettes), cut into 2.5 cm thick slices
8 large scallops with their corals
1 tablespoon olive oil
salt and black pepper
75 ml (2½ fl oz) apple juice
2 tablespoons butter
fresh flat-leaf parsley to garnish
serves 2

1 In separate bowls, place the zucchini slices and scallops. Drizzle each with 2 teaspoons oil, add salt and pepper and toss to coat.

i

preparation time
10 minutes

cooking time
5 minutes

nutritional value per serve
fat: 10.8 g
carbohydrate: 2.6 g
protein: 3.3 g

2 Heat wok to hot on medium high heat. Add the zucchini and stir-fry for 2–3 minutes until lightly browned. Remove to a serving dish and keep hot. Add scallops and stir-fry 1 minute or until just cooked and lightly browned. Add to the zucchini.

3 Pour the apple juice into the wok, add the butter and cook until reduced to a syrupy sauce. Spoon the sauce over the scallops and zucchini slices and garnish with parsley.

mussels with coconut vinegar

ingredients

1.5 kg (3 lb) mussels in their shells
6 whole coriander plants, washed and
    roughly chopped
3 stalks fresh lemon grass, bruised,
    or 1 ½ teaspoons dried lemon grass,
    soaked in hot water until soft
5 cm piece fresh ginger, shredded
½ cup (125 ml, 4 fl oz) water
1 tablespoon vegetable oil
1 red onion, halved and sliced
2 fresh red chillies, sliced
2 tablespoons coconut vinegar
fresh coriander leaves
serves 4

1 Place mussels, coriander, lemon grass, ginger and water in a wok over a high heat. Cover and cook for 5 minutes or until mussels open. Discard any mussels that do not open after 5 minutes cooking. Remove mussels from wok, discard coriander, lemon grass and ginger. Strain cooking liquid and reserve.

2 Heat oil in a wok over a medium heat. Add onion and chillies and stir-fry for 3 minutes or until onion is soft. Add mussels, reserved cooking liquid and coconut vinegar. Stir and toss for 2 minutes or until mussels are heated. Scatter with coriander leaves and serve.

preparation time
5 minutes

cooking time
15 minutes

nutritional value
per serve
fat: 1.7 g
carbohydrate: 3.4 g
protein: 6.6 g

glossary

al dente: Italian term to describe pasta and rice that are cooked until tender but still firm to the bite.

bake blind: to bake pastry cases without their fillings. Line the raw pastry case with greaseproof paper and fill with raw rice or dried beans to prevent collapsed sides and puffed base. Remove paper and fill 5 minutes before completion of cooking time.

baste: to spoon hot cooking liquid over food at intervals during cooking to moisten and flavour it.

beat: to make a mixture smooth with rapid and regular motions using a spatula, wire whisk or electric mixer; to make a mixture light and smooth by enclosing air.

beurre manié: equal quantities of butter and flour mixed together to a smooth paste and stirred bit by bit into a soup, stew or sauce while on the heat to thicken. Stop adding when desired thickness results.

bind: to add egg or a thick sauce to hold ingredients together when cooked.

blanch: to plunge some foods into boiling water for less than a minute and immediately plunge into iced water. This is to brighten the colour of some vegetables; to remove skin from tomatoes and nuts.

blend: to mix 2 or more ingredients thoroughly together; do not confuse with blending in an electric blender.

boil: to cook in a liquid brought to boiling point and kept there.

boiling point: when bubbles rise continually and break over the entire surface of the liquid, reaching a temperature of 100°C (212°F). In some cases food is held at this high temperature for a few seconds then heat is turned to low for slower cooking. See simmer.

bouquet garni: a bundle of several herbs tied together with string for easy removal, placed into pots of stock, soups and stews for flavour. A few sprigs of fresh thyme, parsley and bay leaf are used. Can be purchased in sachet form for convenience.

caramelise: to heat sugar in a heavy-based pan until it liquefies and develops a caramel colour. Vegetables such as blanched carrots and sautéed onions may be sprinkled with sugar and caramelised.

chill: to place in the refrigerator or stir over ice until cold.

clarify: to make a liquid clear by removing sediments and impurities. To melt fat and remove any sediment.

coat: to dust or roll food items in flour to cover the surface before the food is cooked. Also, to coat in flour, egg and breadcrumbs.

cool: to stand at room temperature until some or all heat is removed, eg, cool a little, cool completely.

cream: to make creamy and fluffy by working the mixture with the back of a wooden spoon, usually refers to creaming butter and sugar or margarine. May also be creamed with an electric mixer.

croutons: small cubes of bread, toasted or fried, used as an addition to salads or as a garnish to soups and stews.

crudite: raw vegetable sticks served with a dipping sauce.

crumb: to coat foods in flour, egg and breadcrumbs to form a protective coating for foods which are fried. Also adds flavour, texture and enhances appearance.

cube: to cut into small pieces with six even sides, eg, cubes of meat.

cut in: to combine fat and flour using 2 knives scissor fashion or with a pastry blender, to make pastry.

deglaze: to dissolve dried out cooking juices left on the base and sides of a roasting dish or frying pan. Add a little water, wine or stock, scrape and stir over heat until dissolved. Resulting liquid is used to make a flavoursome gravy or added to a sauce or casserole.

degrease: to skim fat from the surface of cooking liquids, eg, stocks, soups, casseroles.

dice: to cut into small cubes.

dredge: to heavily coat with icing sugar, sugar, flour or cornflour.

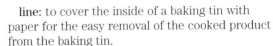

dressing: a mixture added to completed dishes to add moisture and flavour, eg, salads, cooked vegetables.

drizzle: to pour in a fine thread-like stream moving over a surface.

egg wash: beaten egg with milk or water used to brush over pastry, bread dough or biscuits to give a sheen and golden brown colour.

essence: a strong flavouring liquid, usually made by distillation. Only a few drops are needed to flavour.

fillet: a piece of prime meat, fish or poultry which is boneless or has all bones removed.

flake: to separate cooked fish into flakes, removing any bones and skin, using 2 forks.

flame: to ignite warmed alcohol over food or to pour into a pan with food, ignite then serve.

flute: to make decorative indentations around the pastry rim before baking.

fold in: combining of a light, whisked or creamed mixture with other ingredients. Add a portion of the other ingredients at a time and mix using a gentle circular motion, over and under the mixture so that air will not be lost. Use a silver spoon or spatula.

glaze: to brush or coat food with a liquid that will give the finished product a glossy appearance, and on baked products, a golden brown colour.

grease: to rub the surface of a metal or heatproof dish with oil or fat, to prevent the food from sticking.

herbed butter: softened butter mixed with finely chopped fresh herbs and re-chilled. Used to serve on grilled meats and fish.

hors d'ouvre: small savoury foods served as an appetiser, popularly known today as 'finger food'.

infuse: to steep foods in a liquid until the liquid absorbs their flavour.

joint: to cut poultry and game into serving pieces by dividing at the joint.

julienne: to cut some food, eg, vegetables and processed meats into fine strips the length of matchsticks. Used for inclusion in salads or as a garnish to cooked dishes.

knead: to work a yeast dough in a pressing, stretching and folding motion with the heel of the hand until smooth and elastic to develop the gluten strands. Non-yeast doughs should be lightly and quickly handled as gluten development is not desired.

line: to cover the inside of a baking tin with paper for the easy removal of the cooked product from the baking tin.

macerate: to stand fruit in a syrup, liqueur or spirit to give added flavour.

marinade: a flavoured liquid, into which food is placed for some time to give it flavour and to tenderise. Marinades include an acid ingredient such as vinegar or wine, oil and seasonings.

mask: to evenly cover cooked food portions with a sauce, mayonnaise or savoury jelly.

pan-fry: to fry foods in a small amount of fat or oil, sufficient to coat the base of the pan.

parboil: to boil until partially cooked. The food is then finished by some other method.

pare: to peel the skin from vegetables and fruit. Peel is the popular term but pare is the name given to the knife used; paring knife.

pith: the white lining between the rind and flesh of oranges, grapefruit and lemons.

pit: to remove stones or seeds from olives, cherries, dates.

pitted: the olives, cherries, dates etc, with the stone removed, eg, purchase pitted dates.

poach: to simmer gently in enough hot liquid to almost cover the food so shape will be retained.

pound: to flatten meats with a meat mallet; to reduce to a paste or small particles with a mortar and pestle.

simmer: to cook in liquid just below boiling point at about 96°C (205°F) with small bubbles rising gently to the surface.

skim: to remove fat or froth from the surface of simmering food.

stock: the liquid produced when meat, poultry, fish or vegetables have been simmered in water to extract the flavour. Used as a base for soups, sauces, casseroles etc. Convenience stock products are available.

sweat: to cook sliced onions or vegetables, in a small amount of butter in a covered pan over low heat, to soften them and release flavour without colouring.

conversions

easurements differ from country to country, so it's important to understand what the differences are. This Measurements Guide gives you simple 'at-a-glance' information for using the recipes in this book, wherever you may be.

Cooking is not an exact science – minor variations in measurements won't make a difference to your cooking.

equipment

There is a difference in the size of measuring cups used internationally, but the difference is minimal (only 2–3 teaspoons). We use the Australian standard metric measurements in our recipes:

1 teaspoon ....5 ml	1 tablespoon....20 ml
¹/₂ cup......125 ml	1 cup.....250 ml
4 cups...1 litre	

Measuring cups come in sets of one cup (250 ml), ¹/₂ cup (125 ml), ¹/₃ cup (80 ml) and ¹/₄ cup (60 ml). Use these for measuring liquids and certain dry ingredients.
Measuring spoons come in a set of four and should be used for measuring dry and liquid ingredients.
When using cup or spoon measures always make them level (unless the recipe indicates otherwise).

dry versus wet ingredients

While this system of measures is consistent for liquids, it's more difficult to quantify dry ingredients. For instance, one level cup equals: 200 g of brown sugar; 210 g of castor sugar; and 110 g of icing sugar.

When measuring dry ingredients such as flour, don't push the flour down or shake it into the cup. It is best just to spoon the flour in until it reaches the desired amount. When measuring liquids use a clear vessel indicating metric levels.

Always use medium eggs (55–60 g) when eggs are required in a recipe.

dry

metric (grams)	imperial (ounces)
30 g	1 oz
60 g	2 oz
90 g	3 oz
100 g	3 ¹/₂ oz
125 g	4 oz
150 g	5 oz
185 g	6 oz
200 g	7 oz
250 g	8 oz
280 g	9 oz
315 g	10 oz
330 g	11 oz
370 g	12 oz
400 g	13 oz
440 g	14 oz
470 g	15 oz
500 g	16 oz (1 lb)
750 g	24 oz (1¹/₂ lb)
1000 g (1 kg)	32 oz (2 lb)

liquids

metric (millilitres)	imperial (fluid ounces)
30 ml	1 fl oz
60 ml	2 fl oz
90 ml	3 fl oz
100 ml	3 ¹/₂ fl oz
125 ml	4 fl oz
150 ml	5 fl oz
190 ml	6 fl oz
250 ml	8 fl oz
300 ml	10 fl oz
500 ml	16 fl oz
600 ml	20 fl oz (1 pint)*
1000 ml (1 litre)	32 fl oz

*Note: an American pint is 16 fl oz.

oven

Your oven should always be at the right temperature before placing the food in it to be cooked. Note that if your oven doesn't have a fan you may need to cook food for a little longer.

microwave

It is difficult to give an exact cooking time for microwave cooking. It is best to watch what you are cooking closely to monitor its progress.

standing time

Many foods continue to cook when you take them out of the oven or microwave. If a recipe states that the food needs to 'stand' after cooking, be sure not to overcook the dish.

can sizes

The can sizes available in your supermarket or grocery store may not be the same as specified in the recipe. Don't worry if there is a small variation in size—it's unlikely to make a difference to the end result.

cooking temperatures	°C (celsius)	°F (fahrenheit)	gas mark
very slow	120	250	1/2
slow	150	300	2
moderately slow	160	315	2-3
moderate	180	350	4
moderate hot	190	375	5
	200	400	6
hot	220	425	7
very hot	230	450	8
	240	475	9
	250	500	10

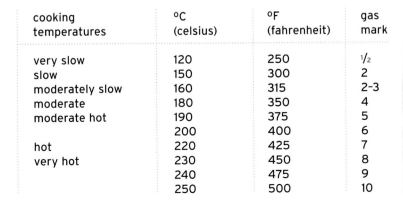

index